"This book is easy reading and yet profound in its message. Bill Gothard has made bare his soul, showing the perspective of a man whose character is a living example of the book's powerful principles."

RAY COMFORT AND KIRK CAMERON,
LIVING WATERS PUBLICATIONS

"The concept of God being a jealous God because He is absolute is a vital truth for the Christian. This book explains the importance of that concept."

DR. SPIROS ZODHIATES, EDITOR IN CHIEF,
THE VOICE OF THE GOSPEL

"I recently read *Our Jealous God* chapter by chapter for evening devotions and was blessed and encouraged. This new book by Bill Gothard led me down the path to a higher level of trust and confidence in my Savior."

JONI EARECKSON TADA, PRESIDENT, JONI AND FRIENDS

OUR JEALOUS GOD

LIFECHANGE BOOKS

BILL GOTHARD

Multnomah® Publishers *Sisters, Oregon*

OUR JEALOUS GOD
published by Multnomah Publishers, Inc.

© 2003 by Institute in Basic Life Principles, Inc.
International Standard Book Number: 1-59052-225-7

Cover image by Veer, Inc./Thomas Francisco

Unless otherwise indicated, Scripture quotations are from:
The Holy Bible, New King James Version
© 1984 by Thomas Nelson, Inc.
Other Scripture quotations are from:
The Holy Bible, King James Version (KJV)
New American Standard Bible® (NASB) © 1960, 1977, 1995
by the Lockman Foundation. Used by permission.
The New Testament in Modern English, Revised Edition (PHILLIPS)
© 1958, 1960, 1972 by J. B. Phillips
Holy Bible, New Living Translation (NLT)
© 1996. Used by permission of Tyndale House Publishers, Inc.
All rights reserved.

Multnomah is a trademark of Multnomah Publishers, Inc.,
and is registered in the U.S. Patent and Trademark Office.
The colophon is a trademark of Multnomah Publishers, Inc.

Printed in the United States of America

For information:
MULTNOMAH PUBLISHERS, INC.
POST OFFICE BOX 1720
SISTERS, OREGON 97759

Library of Congress Cataloging-in-Publication Data

Gothard, Bill.
  Our jealous God / by Bill Gothard.
      p. cm.
  ISBN 1-59052-225-7
  1. Christian life. 2. God—Jealousy. I. Title.
BV4509.5.G65 2003
231'.4—dc21

                                        2003011892

03 04 05 06 07 08—10 9 8 7 6 5 4 3 2 1 0

Dedicated to the further fulfillment of Christ's
prayer in John 17, which will take place as
each member of the Body of Christ
loves the Lord with all of our
heart, soul, mind, and strength,
and our neighbor as ourselves.

"That they may be made perfect in one;
and that the world may know that
thou hast sent me, and hast loved them,
as thou hast loved me."
JOHN 17:23

Table of Contents

ACKNOWLEDGMENTS

I am deeply indebted to the Lord for surrounding me with faithful family, friends, and associates who love the Lord and are committed to serving Him. I am also grateful to the skilled and godly team at Multnomah under the outstanding leadership of Don Jacobson. I am especially grateful for the wise and thorough work of Larry Libby and Thomas Womack, who have brought this book to its present form.

Chapter 1

HIS NAME IS JEALOUS

For you shall worship no other god, for the LORD,
whose name is Jealous, is a jealous God.
EXODUS 34:14

A few days after his marriage, a gregarious young husband decided to demonstrate his love for his bride by taking her out to an elegant restaurant. When they arrived, the maître d' escorted them to a special table and seated them.

Soon the waitress arrived—a bright, attractive young woman. The husband smiled up at her with obvious delight. He noticed her name on her uniform, and used it to engage her in a few moments of spirited conversation.

Then he gave her their order for dinner.

As the waitress walked away, the happy husband turned his eyes back to his wife…and was startled by the change in her countenance. She looked hurt and grieved.

"Honey," he said, "what's wrong?"

"I saw how your eyes lit up when you looked at that waitress. That *hurt* me!"

He was confused. "Hurt you? Why should that hurt you? I was only trying to be friendly. Hey, that's my nature. I'm outgoing. I *enjoy* people."

This distinction did little to comfort his distressed wife. Hadn't he just vowed that "forsaking all others" he would cling to her and be devoted to her? Since their wedding, she had already noticed her husband's eyes brighten up for other women on several occasions—but hadn't said anything until that evening in the restaurant.

Happily, this story has a good ending. The new husband quickly learned his lesson, trained his eyes, and thereafter treated other women in a polite and businesslike way. His eyes still light up—but only when his bride walks into the room. They've gone on to develop a happy and successful marriage.

When I first heard this story, when I heard this young wife explain how hurt and offended she had been with her husband's all-too-evident delight in another woman, I thought to myself, *This lady has a problem with jealousy.*

In my view, it was her problem.

She was obviously overly sensitive, and probably feared being displaced by some other woman. Jealousy, I had always reasoned, was an issue with the one who had it—and he or she needed to work it through.

Just last September, however, I was in a counseling situation that caused me to recall this event…and what transpired on that day changed my life.

That young woman's statement suddenly intruded again into my thoughts; *I saw how your eyes lit up when you looked at that waitress!* In that moment, I saw what I had not seen before: the powerful spiritual significance of those words.

That couple was in a covenant relationship, and in such a union there can be no tolerance of any competing affection. In the wedding ceremony, they both vowed before God that they would cherish each other and love each other with all their hearts.

In this case, the jealousy was warranted. She was right to be jealous. She wanted his eyes. She wanted his heart—his whole heart. And because of their vows, she had every right to expect these things.

Suddenly the words of Scripture leaped into my mind—and stunned me with a whole new meaning.

"For I, the LORD your God, am a jealous God."
EXODUS 20:5

It was one of those pivotal moments when the Spirit of God seems to pull back the curtain, revealing a major truth that was there all along, yet hidden from view. I pondered the meaning of those strong words in Exodus. In what sense was God jealous? Was He only jealous for the nation of Israel—or was He jealous for me, too? What competing affections were there in my own life—words or thoughts or actions—that caused the Almighty Sovereign of the universe to feel the pain of jealousy?

Just as in the case of the jealous bride in that restaurant, God watches the eyes of my heart. He sees whenever my eyes brighten up at some competing affection. His Holy Spirit is grieved by my breach of loyalty. And if I persist in my divided allegiances, I will experience serious conflict in my life, just as that husband and wife experienced on what was supposed to be a joyful evening together.

Someone might comment, "What does the great, omnipotent God care about one of His children being distracted by some passing affection? Surely He has more important things to do than keep track of our small indiscretions or wandering inclinations!"

If we think such thoughts, it is only because we underestimate His love—and His holiness. Scripture shows us that He certainly does notice the little things—the "small" idolatries we so quickly rationalize away. In the book of Jeremiah, the Lord talks to the prophet about a practice among some of the women of Judah. They had been baking little cakes in their ovens—cakes formed in the shape of an idol known as "the queen of heaven" (Jeremiah 44:19).

They were just little flat cakes. We might even stretch the point just a bit and call them cookies. And with all that was going on in the world…with wars and rumors of wars…with all the deliberations of kings and princes and generals…*God was concerned about women baking cookies?*

Yes, He was. Because He knew their hearts. He saw the secret idolatries behind their "innocent" activity. And this is what He said about it:

> "Do you not see what they do in the cities of Judah and in the streets of Jerusalem? The children gather wood, the fathers kindle the fire, and the women knead dough, to make cakes for the queen of heaven; and they pour out drink offerings to other gods, that they may provoke Me to anger."
> JEREMIAH 7:17–18

Those little cakes aroused the jealousy of God, stirring His anger. He noticed…and He was grieved. God clearly states His demand for our total loyalty of love in the first and greatest command: "And you shall love the LORD your God with all your heart, with all your soul, with all your mind, and with all your strength" (Mark 12:30).

After loving the Lord with *all* of our heart, soul, mind,

and strength, there won't be any affection left over for other delights that compete with God.

During that time back in September when the Lord opened my eyes to these things, other Scriptures began to come to mind. I began to ponder the very nature of God. He has many names and titles. One of them, however, isn't much discussed these days. You don't hear of it being made into songs, written in calligraphy on wall plaques, or engraved on Christian jewelry.

And yet, maybe it should be.

It is *Qanna'*.

"Jealous."

In the Ten Commandments He declares, "For I, the LORD your God, am a jealous God" (Exodus 20:5). Several chapters later He states, "The LORD, whose name is Jealous, is a jealous God" (Exodus 34:14). Joshua declared, "He is a holy God. He is a jealous God" (Joshua 24:19).

I'd been aware of such verses, of course, for many years. I'd just assumed they described God's Old Testament relationship with Israel—in a time long ago and a place far away. In the New Testament, I imagined, He became a loving and merciful God who somehow overlooks our competing affections.

The more I considered, however, the more uncomfortable I became with those conclusions. I realized that such thoughts flew in the face of what God Himself declared in

Malachi 3:6: "For I am the LORD, I do not change."

In other words, He was just as loving and merciful in the Old Testament as He is in the New Testament. And He is just as insistent on our total affection and loyalty in the New Testament as He was of His own nation in the Old Testament.

A sense of awe swept over me as I realized that God was aware of every delight, friendship, or affection that was in competition with His character and will for my life. And He was not only aware, but He also cared very deeply about each and every one. To entertain these affections—to return to them and cultivate them in quiet moments of the day or night—was to stir up His jealousy and actually grieve His Holy Spirit, bringing sorrow and conflict into my own life and relationships.

I found myself pleading with God for a fresh measure of His grace and discernment.

If I was making my Lord jealous, I wanted to put an end to it.

POINTS TO PONDER

Are there areas in your life that compete for the affection and loyalty that belong to God alone? Did you ever think of Him as being jealous of those affections of yours? Take these matters to Him in prayer and ask Him to reveal the secrets of your heart.

Chapter 2

LOVING GOD WITH ALL OUR HEART

My son, give me your heart,
and let your eyes observe my ways.
PROVERBS 23:26

One day as a teenager I came across a statement that riveted my attention. It was so intriguing to me that I turned it over and over in my mind for days, pondering its application to my own life.

Now, in retrospect, it seems prophetic.

Be careful what you want when you are fifteen, you will have it when you are thirty. Be careful what you want when you are thirty, you will have it when you are sixty.

When I was fifteen I wanted more than anything to be effective in working with fellow teenagers. When I was thirty, I longed to share what I had learned about young people with a wider audience. It was the great longing of my heart, and God in His grace has fulfilled it.

When we set our heart on something, we begin to fill our eyes and our attention with those things that directly relate to that strong, inner focus. No wonder Scripture warns: "Watch over your heart with all diligence, for from it flow the springs of life" (Proverbs 4:23, NASB). Other priorities, other issues, other events in life which may have great significance to many people escape our notice. Why? Because they don't line up with our goals. They don't match up with the passion of our hearts.

Imagine an athlete, a young man who has been training for years to qualify for the Olympics as a speed skater. Every day of his life he's up before dawn, preparing his body and mind for the competition that fills his waking thoughts. As the week of the Olympic trials finally draws near, how much time does he devote to thinking about other pursuits and interests? He doesn't have time for them!

They're distractions! He is bringing all his energies to bear on one goal: achieving his dream of qualifying for the Olympics.

So it is with loving God as Scripture commands. It is not a casual, halfhearted endeavor. Jesus Himself said we are to love the Lord our God

- with all of our heart,
- with all of our soul,
- with all of our mind, and
- with all of our strength.

Why is this so important? Because our heart is the seat of our affections, *and what we love with our heart shapes the goals and direction of our entire life.* That process, whether we realize it or not, is at work in our lives this very day.

When we become distracted from that pursuit…when we begin to take our eyes off of that goal…when we become immersed in and enchanted by other affections, other "lovers," God is jealous. And rightly so. He is the One who redeemed us, purchasing us at a great and terrible price.

One of my earliest recollections as a young believer is working on projects in the recreation room in my home— and repeating a song over and over.

Into my heart, into my heart;
　　come into my heart, Lord Jesus.

Come in today. Come in to stay.
　　Come into my heart, Lord Jesus.

Now I knew as a young believer that the Lord was
already in my heart—and that He was certainly there to
stay. What I was experiencing, however, was a deeper longing for His presence. I wanted to sense His nearness and
hear His voice. I wanted to know Him *for myself,* not just
as a child of a Christian family or a member of an active
church. It was like a personal response to our Lord's invitation to the Church of Laodicea, "Behold, I stand at the
door and knock. If anyone hears My voice and opens the
door, I will come in to him and dine with him, and he with
Me" (Revelation 3:20).

A number of years ago, I was conducting a counseling
seminar for about eight hundred young people at our
Indianapolis training center. During that week of training,
I received a surprise invitation to meet with the governor of
Indiana. It was a special opportunity, but it required that I
leave one of the sessions half an hour early.

When several students learned about this, they pleaded
with me to let a sixteen-year-old girl named Christiana give
her testimony. With that strong recommendation, I intro-

duced her to the young people and left for my meeting.

As soon as I returned to the auditorium, I sensed something had happened. A marvelous spirit of revival permeated the seminar. There were tears of repentance and joy. I asked what had happened and all they could say was, "We want to love Jesus the way Christiana loves Him."

Christiana expressed her love for the Lord the way most girls express their love for a boyfriend.

She talked about the things He likes.

She boasted about the things He has done.

She shared special things He told her from the Word.

She pointed out mementos of special events with Him and explained the many ways He gave her attention.

Christiana loved the Lord with all her heart...and everyone in the auditorium that day could see it and sense it.

Seek Me with All Your Heart

"You will seek Me and find Me, when you search
for Me with all your heart."
JEREMIAH 29:13

Many have sought the Lord but not found Him because they failed to seek Him with their whole heart.

The challenge of seeking God with our whole heart is

made complicated by the truth of Jeremiah 17:9, "The heart is deceitful above all things, and desperately wicked; who can know it?"

This verse describes the problem: deceit that sends its roots to the very core of our being.

God warns that we have the capacity to hide wrong desires in our heart—to tuck them away in cracks and crevices and behind false panels and hidden doors, secretly hoping that we may one day pull them out and fulfill them. And Satan, perhaps knowing where they are hidden, often provides the perfect opportunities to do just that. People may be shocked when we fall for some illicit desire that seems so out of character, and we too may grieve over the consequences of our own actions. *Yet it is the very thing we secretly wanted to do all along.* The desire was imbedded in our hearts, privately and covertly coddled and nourished for years, waiting for its opportunity.

The only answer to this dilemma is radical surgery.

We must allow the Spirit of God to cut away the covering of our hearts with true repentance and confession, and then cleanse our hearts with the water of the Word.

The capacity of the human heart to hide secret lusts is phenomenal.

Over the years, our ministry has worked with hundreds of troubled youths from various court systems. Many have shown remarkable progress in restoring relationships with parents and growing in their walk with the Lord. If we are not able to help them reveal all the secrets of their hearts, however, they inevitably return to their old ways at the first opportunity. How true the Scripture is, "He who covers his sins will not prosper, but whoever confesses and forsakes them will have mercy" (Proverbs 28:13).

Every one of us must give our heart away to someone or something. If we resist giving it to the Lord and try to keep hidden compartments and corners for ourselves, we only deceive ourselves. And we will face the danger of secret sins taking root in our hearts—sins that may one day lead us into unimaginable heartache and tragedy.

An attractive, seventeen-year-old girl caught the attention and admiration of a nineteen-year-old boy. He found ways to chat with her, and the approval she received from him was beyond anything she had experienced from her own father. That fact alone made her immediately vulnerable to his attention.

The young man obtained her phone number and began calling her at times when her parents weren't at home. It wasn't long before he had stolen her heart. She felt secure in his attention and became more distant from her parents—and also from the Lord. She closed her heart to the conviction of the Holy Spirit, who kept telling her that this friendship was wrong and would hurt her.

When the inevitable confrontation came between the

boy and the girl's parents, the daughter chose the boyfriend and moved out of the house. The father was angry over his daughter's largely secret relationship with the young man. As it turned out, however, she wasn't the only one in the family to practice deception. When the father came in for counseling, he admitted that he was also carrying on a secret friendship with another woman—and had become addicted to pornography.

He wanted his daughter's heart to be turned toward him without deception, yet he had failed to turn His own heart to the Lord without deception. And the simple fact is, *we cannot have what we want without giving God what He wants.*

DELIGHT IN THE LAW OF THE LORD

> Your testimonies also are my delight
> And my counselors....
> Make me walk in the path of Your commandments,
> For I delight in it.
> PSALM 119:24, 35

The process of seeking the Lord with our whole heart really begins with delighting in the Word of God.

In the pages of the Bible, we encounter the living Word of God, Jesus Christ Himself. Jesus told the Jewish leaders, "You search the Scriptures, for in them you think you have eternal life; and these are they which testify of Me" (John 5:39).

Delighting in God has its genesis in reading passages of Scripture and allowing the Holy Spirit to underline, highlight, and apply specific passages. What a wonderful experience that is! Your eyes are scanning a page of the Bible that you have read many, many times. Suddenly a verse seems to stand out as though it was in bold print or highlighted in all the colors of the rainbow. In that moment, the Lord speaks to you through that passage in a very real and timely way. I have marveled time and again at the way the Holy Spirit brings out fresh concepts and new applications from portions of Scripture that I memorized years—even decades—ago.

As I began to engraft these passages into my heart and soul, I found myself understanding—and delighting in—the heart of God as never before. Psalms is an excellent starting point for this experience, because it so poignantly expresses the heart of David, described as a man after God's own heart.

Once as I was reading through the Psalms, I came to Psalm 27:4,

> One thing I have desired of the Lord,
>   That will I seek:
> That I may dwell in the house of the Lord

> All the days of my life,
> To behold the beauty of the LORD,
>   And to inquire in His temple.

I knew immediately this was not true of my heart. I also knew that it *should* be.

So I memorized that verse, and began to put myself to sleep each night quoting it back to the Lord. Each night, I chose a different word to emphasize and to consider how it might apply to my life. This provided an increasingly satisfying fellowship and communion with the Lord. As time went on and I began doing the same thing with other passages of Scripture, I started to see the fulfillment of our Lord's promise in John 15:7–8: "If you abide in Me, and My words abide in you, you will ask what you desire, and it shall be done for you. By this My Father is glorified, that you bear much fruit; so you will be My disciples."

Going to sleep while communing with God through Scripture is a key element to loving Him with all of our heart. The Bible says: "Stand in awe, and sin not: commune with your own heart upon your bed, and be still" (Psalm 4:4, KJV).

During the long years when David fled from Saul in the wilderness of Judah, he composed these words: "When I remember You on my bed, I meditate on You in the night watches. Because You have been my help, therefore in the shadow of Your wings I will rejoice" (Psalm 63:6–7).

Don't think of this as some sort of grim, ironclad discipline. It is sheer delight. As the events of the day and the worries for tomorrow begin to fade from your mind, as your body begins to relax and enjoy the sleep and rest that God intended, your spirit savors those few, last, golden moments of fellowship with the God who loves you. And when you next awaken—whether it's in the middle of the night or with the morning light—that sweet fragrance of God's presence will still be with you.

When I put myself to sleep quoting Scripture, a wonderful cleansing process takes place in my heart and mind. The Word of God cleanses wrong motives, thoughts, and imaginations of the heart, and when the process is completed I have experienced the joy of spiritual dreams, such as talking to people about the Lord and worshiping at the feet of Jesus. When I wake up from these, I experience a whole new love for the Lord and for others.

Day or night, our communion with the Lord will be greatly enhanced as we commit passages to memory. The psalmist declared, "Your word I have hidden in my heart, that I might not sin against You!" (Psalm 119:11).

I've not only enjoyed rich times of fellowship with the Lord as I've put myself to sleep quoting Scripture, I have also planned "night watches," where I wake up in the middle of the night to meditate on God's Word. In the silence and darkness of those hours, I draw near to Him and He draws near to me. It's a comforting reminder of how He is always present with us. Even when we are asleep and unaware, He is there.

Although I was motivated to carry out these pursuits in my teenage years, I often lacked the self-discipline to follow through—especially the getting up early part! To help me reach my goals, I asked others to keep me accountable. Meditation on Scripture became the strongest indicator of my love for the Lord, even as David said in Psalm 104:34, "Let my meditation be sweet to Him; I will be glad in the Lord."

During my elementary school years, I was a very poor student. I actually flunked first grade! The teacher was very tactful in explaining it to me. She called me out into the hall where my mother was waiting, and spoke to me in a bright, enthusiastic voice.

"Well, Billy, how would you like to be a *leader* in first grade, by going through it again next year?"

A second time through first grade, however, didn't help too much. Because I was getting rather large for the chairs, they passed me on probation. Every year thereafter, I was passed on probation.

After elementary school, one of my older sisters groaned aloud at the prospect of my going to high school.

"What's your problem?" I asked her.

"You'll be getting poor grades," she exclaimed, "and pretty soon we'll become known as sisters of a dumbbell!"

That encounter lit a small fire under me, motivating me to work hard for better grades. I spent hours every night toiling away on homework. The best I could manage, however, try as I might, was just a little above "C-level." Then one day a godly older woman at church asked if I would like to be successful in life. Her question caught me a little off guard, but I didn't have to think long about the answer. I gave her a definite yes, and she challenged me to memorize a large passage of Scripture every week and quote it to her.

It took about seventeen hours a week to accomplish this, because I was such a poor learner. When my grades came out the next semester, however, they averaged A-. Every year thereafter, my grades improved in direct proportion to my faithfulness in memorizing and meditating on Scripture. Everyone was surprised, including me, when I graduated from high school in the National Honor Society and from college with honors.

Thousands of others have experienced similar results. One medical student of average academic ability began memorizing chapters of Scripture. He graduated from medical school in the ninetieth percentile. In graduate school, he was in the ninety-fifth percentile, and on the final national testing, he ranked in the ninety-ninth percentile. He attributes this directly to his diligence in meditation on God's Word.

MOVING TOWARD MATURITY

God wants each of His children to be moving down life's road toward a "perfect heart."

What does that mean? That we will never sin?

No, the apostle assures us that we do sin and will sin. John wrote: "If we say that we have no sin, we deceive ourselves, and the truth is not in us. If we confess our sins, He is faithful and just to forgive us our sins and to cleanse us from all unrighteousness. If we say that we have not sinned, we make Him a liar, and His word is not in us" (1 John 1:8–10).

Sinless perfection isn't possible this side of heaven. Even Paul acknowledged that he tried to reach this status—but wasn't able to (Philippians 3:12–14).

He admitted candidly that he was aiming for perfection—but wasn't there yet. But that didn't mean he would stop trying! Refusing to allow yesterday's failures to discourage him or tomorrow's challenges to intimidate him, he would make it his life goal to strain and press toward the mark.

Scripture urges all of us to mature in our walk with the Lord—and especially in our love for others.

This "telos" perfection is explained in Ephesians 4:13: "Till we all come to the unity of the faith and of the knowledge of the Son of God, to a perfect [telos] man, to the measure of the stature of the fullness of Christ."

That's a long way to go and a long way to grow. It is a step-by-step journey enabled by the gift of God's grace and the faith that He gives to every believer.

In fact, God is jealous that we walk in this direction— hour by hour, day by day, year by year.

POINTS TO PONDER

Are you willing to allow the Great Physician to perform radical heart surgery in your life? As you read and meditate on Scripture, ask the Holy Spirit to reveal any secret corners or private closets that you have never fully yielded to Him.

Chapter 3

LOVING GOD
WITH ALL
OUR SOUL

The law of the LORD is perfect,
converting the soul.
PSALM 19:7

As a teenager, Doug was plagued with doubts about God and the Bible.

"But how do we *know* that God is real?" he would ask me. "How can we be *sure* that the Bible is true?"

As he pressed me for answers, I finally replied, "Doug, even if I answered *all* your questions—right now, this minute—it wouldn't help you. It's clear to me that you have exalted your own mind above God's Word and God's Spirit. Only as you bring your mind, will, and emotions under God's authority will you understand the answers to your questions."

That was a new thought to Doug.

He wasn't aware that he'd placed his mind above God's Word and Spirit. Yet that is the sure result when we depend upon our human reasoning to understand the deep truths of Scripture. These great principles are not intellectually understood as much as they are spiritually discerned.

And this is the very message of Scripture. "For what man knows the things of a man except the spirit of the man which is in him? Even so no one knows the things of God except the Spirit of God" (1 Corinthians 2:11). The knowledge we acquire with human reasoning tends to puff us up, and in our pride we think that we can fully understand God and the Bible.

I asked Doug if he had ever consciously taken his mind, will, and emotions off the throne and brought them under the jurisdiction of God's Holy Spirit and God's Word. He said that he hadn't, and I urged him to take that step right then. He agreed—but his soul did not surrender without a battle.

In his first attempt, Doug prayed, "O God, I know my

mind and will are on the throne, and—I want to take them off. Amen."

He opened his eyes and looked over at me.

"Doug, you just told God that you *want* to take your mind and will off the throne. Now let's *do* it."

He prayed again. "Lord, help me to take my mind and will off the throne of my life. Amen."

"Doug," I said gently, "God will help you. He wants to help you. But this is something you must do with an act of your mind, will, and emotions. You must say with sincerity, 'God, I do now take my mind, will, and emotions off the throne of my life and I place Your Spirit and Your Word in that place. From now on, You are in control of my thoughts, emotions, and decisions.'"

In his own words, Doug prayed those concepts to the Lord. After he finished, something unexpected took place. All those questions that had plagued him for so long suddenly seemed unimportant! He now had a spiritual discernment that gave him a new perspective on God, the Bible, and all of life.

Paul explained the conflict of human reasoning with spiritual discernment when he wrote, "For you see your calling, brethren, that not many wise according to the flesh, not many mighty, not many noble, are called" (1 Corinthians 1:26).

Jesus said of deep spiritual truth, "I thank You, Father, Lord of heaven and earth, that You have hidden these things from the wise and prudent and revealed them to babes" (Luke 10:21). Only those who have childlike faith in an infinitely wise God will comprehend these things. For "the natural man does not receive the things of the Spirit of God, for they are foolishness to him; nor can he know them, because they are spiritually discerned" (1 Corinthians 2:14).

Have you felt your hope and joy beginning to flag lately? Spiritual discernment through the commands of Christ allows us to look beyond our present prospects and circumstances to see those exceedingly great "things which God has prepared for those who love Him."

CONVERTING OUR SOUL WITH GOD'S LAW

Scripture tells us that "the law of the LORD is perfect, converting the soul" (Psalm 19:7). When we become a believer, our spirit is born again. Our soul, however, must be converted as well. The word *convert* means to turn around, to totally change our direction. This is what the Law of God does to our souls with great rewards.

God promised Joshua that he would have "good success" in leadership and warfare if he kept the law before him and meditated on it day and night (Joshua 1:8). The testimony of Psalm 119 is equally significant:

Oh, how I love Your law!
    It is my meditation all the day.
You, through Your commandments,
    make me wiser than my enemies;
for they are ever with me.
    I have more understanding than all my teachers,
for Your testimonies are my meditation.

vv. 97–99

Jesus clarified the law in the commands He taught to His disciples, and it is by keeping the commandments of Christ before our eyes—with the goal of doing them—that we demonstrate our love for Him. Jesus said. "If you love Me, keep My commandments" (John 14:15).

The commands of Jesus not only convert our mind, will, and emotions, but they also reveal to us who the Lord really is. No wonder Paul exhorts "Let the word of Christ dwell in you richly in all wisdom" (Colossians 3:16). And James commands, "In humility receive the word implanted, which is able to save your souls" (James 1:21, NASB).

CONTROLLING OUR SOUL WITH FASTING

Someone has described the Christian life as a pitched battle between two dogs. When a spectator asked which dog would win, the one in charge said, "Whichever one I feed!"

Paul said this in another way, "For the flesh sets its

desire against the Spirit, and the Spirit against the flesh; for these are in opposition to one another, so that you may not do the things that you please…. For the one who sows to his own flesh will from the flesh reap corruption, but the one who sows to the Spirit will from the Spirit reap eternal life" (Galatians 5:17, 6:8, NASB).

Paul was also very aware of the need to control the desires and appetites of his soul with personal disciplines. He compared himself to a runner who was intent on winning the prize: "But I discipline my body and bring it into subjection, lest, when I have preached to others, I myself should become disqualified" (1 Corinthians 9:27).

One of the main elements of Paul's program of self-control was fasting. He affirms that he was "in fastings often" (2 Corinthians 11:27).

I still vividly remember the first time I tried to go without food for a whole day. The idea came to me as I was memorizing the words of Jesus, "But you, when you fast, anoint your head and wash your face, so that you do not appear to men to be fasting, but to your Father who is in the secret place; and your Father who sees in secret will reward you openly" (Matthew 6:17–18).

A little room in my church provided the setting for my spiritual "adventure." With my Bible, a notebook, and a hymnal, I began. After what seemed like hours, I went into the next room to check the clock. It told me told me that I had been fasting for less than an hour!

Those who fast experience this phenomena; the clock seems to slow down. So, if you want to get more done—just fast!

In a few hours my stomach announced that it was lunchtime. Now I had a new challenge to contend with. As I tried to read the Bible, my mind would visualize sizzling steaks, creamy chocolate ice cream, and thick milk shakes. My soul said to my spirit, "Congratulations! You've fasted. Now let's get something to eat!" But my spirit objected, so I continued the fast.

After several more hours and battles with my flesh, an exciting new experience began for me. In a way I'd never known before in my young life, God opened the rich treasures of His truth to my spiritual understanding and showed me how to apply them to my life. The spiritual rewards of that day motivated me to repeat this on a weekly basis.

Over and over again, Scripture affirms open rewards for secret fasting. Ezra fasted and prayed for safety from marauding robbers and God protected them (Ezra 8:21–23). Nehemiah fasted and confessed the sins of the plundered people of God in Jerusalem, and God gave him a winning strategy (Nehemiah 1:4).

The elders of the church at Antioch ministered to the

Lord and fasted, and God instructed them to send out Paul and Barnabas to reach the Gentile world (Acts 13:2–3). When God wants to do something special in my life or ministry, He calls me to a time of fasting.

SOMETHING SPECIAL

One Sunday morning, I woke up with a clear sense that I should fast that day. But I had a problem. I had already agreed to a dinner engagement with a godly couple in a neighboring town. How could I honor my promise to be with them and still honor the Lord in fasting?

After church I drove to their home. They gave me a warm welcome and then I said, "I need to tell you something that's very difficult to explain." They asked what it was, and I said, "This morning God made it very clear to me that I should spend the day in fasting, but I want to honor my commitment to be with you, so if you would allow me to just skip the eating part, we can still have fellowship and I'll be just fine." They understood immediately and let me know that I must follow the Lord's leading. "We can have a meal together at another time," they said. "You go home and be with the Lord."

The Lord honored that day of fasting in a startling way during the following week. Every evening, I had been meeting with various neighborhood gangs in Chicago—but without seeing any spiritual results. On Monday evening, on the way to meet with a south-side gang, I saw two young men in leather jackets hitchhiking alongside the road. I pulled over and motioned for them to get in the car.

As we drove on, I asked them where they lived. "In the area," they mumbled.

I turned to the young man sitting next to the door and said, "What's your name?" He gave me his last name and almost spontaneously, I said, "Is your first name Bill?"

He looked at me with a fearful curiosity. "Yes," he said.

I turned to the other fellow sitting next to me and asked for his name. He also gave me his last name. I sent up a quick prayer. *Lord, what's his first name?* The name Tom came to my mind. So I asked, "Is your first name Tom?"

They both looked at me in amazement. The second young man blurted out, "How do you know our names? Are you a cop?" I was actually as surprised as they were and said, "Is your name really Tom?" He lifted up his left arm and pushed his coat sleeve back. There on his arm were the tattooed letters, T-o-m.

"Bill and Tom," I said, "Listen to me. I've never guessed names like this before in my life. Obviously, God wants you to know that what I have to say to you next is as true and important as your names."

After I explained the gospel to them, they admitted that they were actually running away from home to go to California. I immediately realized that my ability to tell them their names—and their response to the gospel—was a direct result of God preparing my heart through fasting. Throughout the rest of the week many gang members who had been resisting the gospel called upon the Lord for salvation.

When I approached the age of thirty, the thought came to my mind, *Jesus fasted for forty days when He reached this age—why couldn't I do the same?* The idea became exciting to me, and toward the end of a dark, cold December, I traveled to a Northwoods lodge for what became the turning point of my life.

During those precious weeks, the temperature plunged to thirty to forty degrees below zero outside with snow drifts up to five feet deep. It was also chilly in my upstairs room, but I was experiencing an intimacy with the Lord that I had never known before. I wrote out the lessons God had taught me during the previous fifteen years of working with youth and their parents. This material became the textbook of the Basic Youth Conflicts Seminar, attended by millions over the last thirty plus years.

One of my goals during the Northwoods retreat was to read through the entire Bible. As I came to Psalm 21, I had a personal experience with the Lord that has impacted my life since. "The king shall have joy in Your strength, O LORD; and in Your salvation how greatly shall he rejoice!" (v. 1).

That truth prepared me for the next verse. "You have given him his heart's desire, and have not withheld the request of his lips" (v. 2).

In that moment, I had an unusual awareness that God was inviting me to make a request of Him. I remembered how pleased God was with the request of Solomon. I also wanted wisdom—but something more, too. I desired to experience God's way of life, and to have the ability to explain it to others so that they would also understand it.

I asked the Lord to give me His life, and the ability to teach it to others. Then I looked down to continue reading. My eyes fell on verse four and a thrill shot through my whole being. "He asked life from You, and You gave it to him" (v. 4).

Following that time in the Northwoods, I was invited to teach a summer course at Wheaton College. They named the class "Basic Youth Conflicts." The first class had forty-five pastors, youth directors, and college students. The next year one hundred and twenty enrolled. And then there were one thousand; then ten thousand, and soon up to twenty-eight thousand in a single thirty-two-hour seminar. Truly, God had begun to fulfill the promise of 1 Corinthians 2:9:

> Eye has not seen, nor ear heard,
> Nor have entered into the heart of man
> The things which God has prepared for those who
> love Him.

What special thing does God want to do through you?

What lives does He want you to touch in His name?

What doors—beyond your imagination—does He want to open for you?

What portion of this darkened world does He want to illuminate through the lamp of your life, held high?

Yes, He certainly has incomprehensible things planned for us in heaven, through the endless days of eternity. But He also has plans to use you in His service in this life—in these brief days before we all stand together in His presence. And He *will* use those who have loved Him with all of their soul—offering body, mind, emotions, and will wholeheartedly to Him.

In fact, He is *jealous* for that to happen.

And it is the jealousy of infinite love.

POINTS TO PONDER

If you've never tried fasting, consider how this discipline might move you down the path to loving Him with all your soul. You might begin with a single day—or even a single meal—and use that time to seek your Father in the secret place. Be sure to check with your doctor before attempting an extended fast of weeks, as I described.

Chapter 4

LOVING GOD
WITH ALL
OUR MIND

And be renewed in the spirit of your mind.
EPHESIANS 4:23

I once heard of a simple test to determine what I truly love most in life. It went like this:

- When I get a free moment, what do I enjoy thinking about the most?
- What is my last thought before going to sleep at night?

- What is my first thought upon waking up in the morning?

Our thoughts, of course, pass through a maze of memories, impressions, and imaginations—the picture gallery of the mind, with miles of walls and countless photographs. Some of the pictures are sharp and distinct, others fuzzy and half developed—hardly more than a vague image or a blur. Some of the pictures we've hardly noticed or thought about for years; others we came back to again and again.

The pictures may include the home of our dreams, shots of sports heroes or entertainers, sketches of future plans—or lewd and pornographic images we've encountered through the years. God sees them all and knows exactly which ones we delight in.

And He is jealous for those thoughts of ours. He is well aware of which pictures we return to again and again and where we allow our attentions to linger.

The book of Ezekiel gives us a graphic picture of God's constant awareness of our inmost thoughts. In one of the prophet's amazing visions, God transports him to the temple in Jerusalem. He tells Ezekiel to dig through the temple wall and see what the elders of Israel were gazing upon in the secrecy of their minds.

So I went in and saw, and there—every sort of creeping thing, abominable beasts, and all the idols of the house of Israel, portrayed all around on the walls. And there stood before them seventy men of the elders of the house of Israel…. Then He said to me, "Son of man, have you seen what the elders of the house of Israel do in the dark, every man in the room of his idols? For they say, 'The LORD does not see us, the LORD has forsaken the land.'"

EZEKIEL 8:10–12

But the Lord did see, didn't He? And so did His prophet. And so have the millions upon millions of people who have read this account in Scripture. There is no such thing as secret sin.

Once we etch a picture on one of the walls of our mind, it is extremely difficult to remove. Especially one that fulfills the lusts of the flesh or the mind. The fallacy of these lustful images is that they are deceitful—not at all true to life. Their promise of pleasure is empty. When I worked with the gangs in the city of Chicago, I remember encountering provocatively dressed girls having promiscuous relationships with young men. I found that I could not describe what I had seen to the people who were praying for my ministry. To do so would have created scenes of impurity in the minds of those who read my prayer letters. A person might imagine something to be exciting or sensual, but what I saw was ugliness and despair.

It's the same with pornography. The images may promise beauty or glamour, but it is a lie. The smell of death clings to them.

For this reason, Solomon warned his son, "Do not lust after her beauty in your heart, nor let her allure you with her eyelids. For by means of a harlot a man is reduced to a crust of bread; and an adulteress will prey upon his precious life" (Proverbs 6:25–26). In other words, pornography will eat you alive; it will take you right down to nothing.

The fact is, any pleasures that we picture in our minds that are contrary to the will of God are iniquity, and it was for our iniquities that Jesus died on the cross. For this reason, I have found it very effective to superimpose the picture of Jesus—brutally beaten and dripping with blood—over every picture in my mind that was not righteous, and to quote the Scripture, "But He was wounded for our transgressions, He was bruised for our iniquities" (Isaiah 53:5).

How can I linger over images that caused my Lord to be wounded, bruised, and crushed?

The next important step is to cleanse my mind with Scripture even as Jesus instructed, "You are already clean because of the word which I have spoken to you," (John 15:3) and "Sanctify them by Your truth. Your word is truth" (John 17:17).

When our minds are cleansed of evil and filled with

God's Word, we are able to experience the instructions of Paul: "Stand fast in one spirit, with one mind striving together for the faith of the gospel" (Philippians 1:27). We are also able to enjoy the reward of Philippians 4:7: "The peace of God, which surpasses all understanding, will guard your hearts and minds through Christ Jesus."

The word that Jesus used in the command to "love God with all our...mind" (Mark 12:30) is *dianoia*. It means a "thinking through, or a meditation." It involves a moral reflection based on knowing or understanding and has a direct bearing on the renewing of our mind through the Holy Spirit: "Do not be conformed to this world, but be transformed by the renewing of your mind, that you may prove what is that good and acceptable and perfect will of God" (Romans 12:2). One paraphrase of this verse says, "Don't let the world around you squeeze you into its own mold, but let God remold your minds from within."[1]

In view of this, we might even add one more question to that three-question test with which we opened this chapter. *What am I allowing to mold my mind—the outside pressures of the world or the inside power of the indwelling Christ?*

Loving the Lord with all my mind means bringing every thought and imagination into conformity with the teachings of the Lord Jesus Christ. The grace that God gives to us to do this is a mighty weapon against the moral attacks on our mind. Paul stated, "For the weapons of our warfare are not carnal but mighty in God for pulling down strongholds" (2 Corinthians 10:4).

WHATEVER IT COSTS

Ken knew by firsthand experience how powerful the lusts of the mind can become. From age fourteen, he had daily bouts with lustful thoughts and tried everything he knew to overcome them. He prayed, read his Bible, fasted, and memorized Scripture, but nothing seemed to work for very long.

The battles continued for years, and Ken thought, *Surely after I get married that problem will be out of my life and I will have victory.* Yet marriage did not solve his problems. I've been told that in some ways, marriage and sexual experience makes the battle with lustful thoughts even more intense.

Ken studied for the ministry and became a pastor. But he often felt guilty for the moral battles he lost in his mind, will, and emotions. One day at a seminar, he learned about regaining the "ground" he had surrendered to Satan in his soul. He did not fully understand the biblical concepts behind it, but on his two-hour drive home, he decided to try it.

He asked the Lord to bring back to mind every moral defeat. He confessed each one, claimed the blood of Christ for full forgiveness, and asked God to take back the ground he had surrendered into Satan's control. During this personal cleansing, the Lord reminded him of an event in his early life during which he opened himself up to impurity. He confessed that sin and then cried out to the Lord with the words, *"Oh God! Give me victory, whatever it costs!"*

From that day, God did give him victory over his mind, will, and emotions in the area of moral impurity. The "cost" was going before his church and confessing that he had viewed pornography on the Internet. Many came forward to assure him of their forgiveness and to thank him for being honest so that they could follow his example.

Today, Ken has a close walk with the Lord. His mind is cleansed by the blood of Christ and the Word of God, and he is having a profound ministry in the lives of others.

Loving God with all of our mind means bringing our thoughts into alignment with His. It means seeing life as He sees life. Viewing opportunities as He views opportunities. Hating sin as He hates sin.

Only the Word of God, illumined for us by the Spirit of God, can accomplish this in our minds. Paul told Timothy that "all Scripture is given by inspiration of God, and is profitable for doctrine, for reproof, for correction, for instruction in righteousness, that the man of God may be complete, thoroughly equipped for every good work" (2 Timothy 3:16–17).

One paraphrase of this verse speaks about "re-setting

the direction of a man's life and training him in good living."2

That's the effect of God's Word on our minds. Like an internal compass, it resets our direction and turns us toward God's desired outcomes in our lives. Jesus said, "If you love Me, keep My commandments" (John 14:15).

The word *keep* means "to set before our eyes and guard for use." It is explained by the expression of navigators who say they "keep the stars," which means they keep their course by the stars in the heavens. God gives us a marvelous promise if we do this. "He who has My commandments and keeps them, it is he who loves Me. And he who loves Me will be loved by My Father, and I will love him and manifest Myself to him" (John 14:21).

When we begin to honor and obey the commands of Christ and keep them foremost in our thoughts, we will steer our lives away from the shoals and reefs that could sink us, and toward destinations that will delight us beyond our imagination.

POINTS TO PONDER

How did you do on the three-question test at the beginning of this chapter? What step would it take in your life to make the Lord foremost in all your thoughts? Be willing to seek regular accountability from a Christian friend.

Chapter 5

LOVING GOD
WITH ALL OUR
STRENGTH

If you faint in the day of adversity,
your strength is small.
PROVERBS 24:10

One Friday afternoon back in my junior college days, I walked into my history classroom a few minutes early and sat down at my desk. Only a few other students were present, along with the professor, Dr. Kenyon, who sat at his desk in front of the room.

He seemed to be deep in thought as he looked down at his desk. Dr. Kenyon was one of my favorite teachers. His slender build and white hair were impressive. He was a gentle and articulate instructor, without a trace of arrogance. He had a kind face and humble manner.

Suddenly, he stood up and began walking down the aisle toward me. When he got to me, he placed a piece of notebook paper on my desk. I picked it up and read the handwritten words: "Why does God waste energy on us when we are young, and wisdom on us when we are old?"

I looked up at Dr. Kenyon and was startled by his pleading, searching expression. With a start, I realized that he was expecting an answer about the meaning of life…and he was hoping I would give it to him!

I later thought through how I should have answered his question. I should have said, "We are to call upon the Lord in our youth for salvation and dedicate our strength to Him, so that when we are older and wiser, we can teach others about His love and truth."

I should have had an answer. I should have been ready to explain the hope that I possessed, as it says in 1 Peter 3:15. But I didn't have the answer and I wasn't ready. Instead, I mumbled some insignificant, offhand comment, feeling my face grow hot with embarrassment. Dr. Kenyon waited for what seemed like several minutes, his eyes imploring me for an answer. When he realized I didn't have anything else to say to him, he slowly turned around and walked back to his desk.

During the lecture that day, my heart and mind were racing. I could think only about the opportunity I had missed. I was both honored and overwhelmed that he would ask me for such an answer. I made up my mind to come in after my classes that day and talk to him. At the end of the day, however, I got involved in other matters. By the time I got back to his classroom, he was gone. Feeling a sudden urgency to talk with him, I decided to find out where he lived and visit him at his house.

My intentions were good, but other activities during the weekend crowded out this goal. I told myself I would talk to him for sure on Monday. But as I walked up to his classroom, a group of students stood in front of his bulletin board. I approached the group with a knot in my stomach. A notice on the board stated that Dr. Kenyon would not be teaching this class. Never again would he teach his history class—because he had passed away!

I was crushed in my spirit and grieved for the lack of energy I had expended to share the gospel with an earnest inquirer. I can still see those searching eyes of his. I have no idea what his spiritual condition might have been, but the words of Ezekiel took on new meaning for me that day. "When I say to the wicked, 'You shall surely die,' and you give him no warning, nor speak to warn the wicked from his wicked way, to save his life, that same wicked man shall die in his iniquity; but his blood I will require at your hand" (Ezekiel 3:18).

So many activities that sap our strength and drain our energies will have no eternal value. For this reason, God warns us to be "redeeming the time, because the days are evil" (Ephesians 5:16).

TWO VITAL QUESTIONS

Before I entered high school, a youth leader named Jack Hamilton invited me to drive with him to a conference in Kansas City. This turned out to be one of the most significant trips of my life. Along the way, he explained a new idea he'd been working on to get young people into the Bible. He called it "Bible Quizzing," a method that went on to be used for years by thousands of churches.

At one point in the trip, he turned to me and said, "Bill, did you ever see the truth of Psalm 127:1? 'Unless the LORD builds the house, they labor in vain who build it.' Notice that in both cases, the house is built, but in one case it is in vain."

Stunned by that insight, I made up my mind that whatever I did for the Lord would be directed by Him.

Jack then gave me some counsel that impacted the rest of my life. "Bill, when you get to high school, ask yourself two questions before you get involved in any extracurricular activities. First ask, 'Will this activity count ten years from now?' Second, 'Will this activity count for eternity?' Those two questions are like the markers that help a farmer plow a straight furrow. An experienced plowman will pick a post at the end of the field—and then a distant tree behind it. As long as those two markers line up, he knows he's heading in a straight line."

During the meetings that followed, I was challenged to present the gospel to every student in my high school. Each year, I made this my goal and gave all my energies to it. One year, I conducted a phone poll asking fellow students what they thought were the most important things in life.

Following the phone poll, I sent each a letter thanking him or her for taking part in the poll. I then expressed my desire that each student would discover the single most important thing in life, and enclosed a booklet for that purpose. It was titled "The Most Important Thing in Life." Its message was straightforward and simple: What matters most in life is not money, sports, education, or entertainment, but knowing Jesus Christ as Savior.

I was so busy with these projects and memorizing Scripture that I only had time to attend part of a football game during my four years in high school. My role model was the apostle Paul who summed up his life to the church at Colosse: "So naturally, we proclaim Christ! We warn everyone we meet, and we teach everyone we can, all that we know about him, so that we may bring every man up to his full maturity in Christ. This is what I am working and struggling at with all the strength that God puts into me."[3]

When I think of that focused energy, I'm reminded of Dave, a high school student who assisted me for several years in my youth work. When Dave tried out for the track team as a sophomore, his coach immediately recognized running ability and signed him up.

Meanwhile, Dave proved to be an able assistant to me and very effective with teenagers. As he worked with other teens, God also worked on his heart. He began to consider what ought to be first place in his life—track or the Lord. Dave felt impressed that God was asking him to place his abilities, time, and talents on the altar. So one day he made the very difficult decision to quit the track team.

When he told his coach that he had to drop out of the team for personal reasons, the coach urged him to go and talk to another track coach named Gil Dodds. Gil had achieved fame by holding the world's record for the indoor mile for four years. When Gil Dodds signed his autograph, he would often add the Scripture reference Philippians 4:13: "I can do all things through Christ who strengthens me." (Many fans would look curiously at "Phil. 4:13" and assume it meant he'd run a four minute and thirteen second mile in Philadelphia!)

Gil Dodds understood Dave's spiritual battle, and encouraged him in his decision to put God first. With this confirmation in his heart, Dave returned to his coach and finalized his resignation from the team. After this decision, Dave felt a tremendous burden lifted from him. But then something unexpected happened. It was as if God said to Dave, "Now that I know I am in first place, you can go back to the team." So he surprised and delighted the coach by returning.

The test of "first place" came one weekend when Dave had to choose between assisting at a youth retreat and competing in an important track meet. He decided to be at the youth retreat when it began on Friday evening, and then try to make it back for the race on Saturday afternoon. When he arrived at the meet, the coach motioned him to quickly change and get in the race. He joined his competitors at the starting blocks, and the race began. Dave pulled ahead of all the other runners and broke the tape with wild cheering ringing in his ears.

God honored Dave's decision to put Him first by allowing him to excel in track through his high school and college days. As an associate pastor of a large suburban church, Dave continues to experience his Lord's blessing. To this very day, Dave has kept his eyes focused on the goal of pleasing Christ…and still attempts to run the race with all his strength.

POINTS TO PONDER

What activities and commitments in your life keep you from loving and serving Christ with all your strength? Ask yourself: "Will my involvement in these things make any difference ten years from now...or in eternity?"

Chapter 6

COMPETING AFFECTION #1: LOVING OUR LIFE

Set your mind on things above, not on things on the earth.
For you died, and your life is hidden
with Christ in God.
COLOSSIANS 3:2–3

The doctor looked into his patient's eyes.

"I'll give it to you straight. I'm terribly sorry to tell you this, but you will not be getting better. This illness will take your life within six months—and there's nothing we can do."

The man received this shocking news calmly. *We all have to die sometime,* he reasoned. But what he didn't want was some ordinary, garden-variety death. He wanted a dramatic end to his life that would accomplish something significant.

Several days later, he came across an amazing scene—scores of police surrounded a convenience store in his neighborhood. Inside, an armed robber held several hostages.

The man went up to the police captain and said he wanted to go into the store and talk to the gunman. The officer immediately objected. "You're crazy, mister. You'll be killed!"

"That's exactly what I want," the man replied. "I only have a few months to live anyway."

Eventually, lacking other options, the police allowed the man to go into the store. With no fear of death, he approached the gunman directly. His boldness caused the robber to panic. Thinking there must be some imminent plan to rush the store and capture him, the felon surrendered.

The man on borrowed time calmly pocketed the weapon and walked out of the store with the gunman and his hostages. The crowd cheered and the man became an instant hero.

But he still had his dilemma.

A few days later, he heard about a riot raging in a nearby prison. He rushed over and volunteered to go in to talk to the rioters. "You can't do that," the guards told him. "They'll kill you!"

"That's what I'm hoping will happen," the man replied, "because I'm going to die in a few months anyway. You may as well let me go in and see if I can save a few lives."

Reluctantly, the guards pushed him through the gate and locked it behind him. Astonished that an unarmed man would simply walk in and talk to them, the prisoners listened to what he had to say and decided to stop their rioting. The man was again a hero...but he still wondered how he was going to accomplish his goal.

Then one day he received a call from his doctor. "I have good news for you! I misdiagnosed your case. You're not going to die after all!" Just that quickly, the man lost all his extraordinary courage and returned to his normal fearful self.

While I cannot document this account, I can verify the following report—which affirms the fact that the most powerful people on the face of the earth are those who have no fear of death.

Dr. Josef Tson lived during the communist rule of the Romanian dictator, Nicolae Ceausescu. He wrote a paper on the truth of Christianity and the deception of Communism, and personally delivered a copy to the dictator's office. A short time later (and right on cue), a police car pulled up in front of his home and Dr. Tson was arrested. At the police station they demanded he retract what he had written. He couldn't do that, he told the officers, for the simple reason that it was the truth.

"If you don't take back what you have written," they told him, "we will kill you!" Dr. Tson just stood there with a peaceful smile.

"Don't you realize what we just said?" they raged. "You're going to die!"

"If you kill me," he replied, "you will force me to use my weapon against you."

Taken aback, they asked him, "What is your weapon?"

"To die for my faith," he said. "For many years, I have been preaching the gospel throughout Romania. Thousands of people have my messages on tape. When they hear that I have died for my faith, they will listen to my messages with new determination. Would you please kill me?"

Realizing the truth of what he had just told them, they decided not to execute Dr. Tson. Instead, they interrogated him for months and then let him go. Several years ago, the top officials of this very organization met with us at our Indianapolis Training Center and worked out a written agreement for us to train one hundred thousand of their police officials, which we're in the process of doing.

Scripture states that the saints overcome Satan "by the blood of the Lamb and by the word of their testimony, and that they did not love their lives to the death" (Revelation 12:11). When Jesus called His disciples to follow Him, He challenged them to a life of self-sacrifice and a death of martyrdom. Most of His disciples were in fact martyred for their faith. Yet it was through their death that tens of thousands of others became believers.

The Roman empire was conquered by the martyrs who were then given a crown of life. During the great persecutions in the first centuries, an official rushed into the emperor and said, "Stop burning these Christians! Their smoke causes everyone in the crowd to become believers."

Jesus sounded the challenge, "If anyone desires to come after Me, let him deny himself, and take up his cross, and follow Me. For whoever desires to save his life will lose it, but whoever loses his life for My sake will find it" (Matthew 16:24–25).

One of the most important events of my life took place when I was about thirteen years old. The surroundings are vivid in my memory to this day. I was sitting at the window of my bedroom reading *Foxe's Book of Martyrs*. As I leafed through those pages, I tried to imagine the excruciating pain those believers endured by having their limbs pulled out of their bodies on the rack or being boiled in oil or burned at the stake.

I was especially impressed with John Huss, who as a boy lit a candle and put his finger over the flame to see if he was courageous enough to be burned at the stake—which is exactly what happened years later.

At that important moment of my life, I sensed the Lord asking me, *Bill, will you also die for Me?* With all my sincerity and resolve, I responded that I would die for Him. Something happened within me as I made that resolution. I pictured myself in a race against time. How much could I get done for the Lord before I died for Him? From that moment, I began to care less and less about a fun-filled life, and more and more about a fruitful death.

MY LIFE FOR HIS

Purposing to die for the Lord is a good starting point. I soon learned, however, that God does not usually call us to a dramatic martyrdom, but rather to a daily dying to self. Losing my life was a moment to moment process of choosing those things that would please the Lord and advance His kingdom and rejecting those things that would gratify my desires and hinder the work of the Lord.

A great deal of our life is wrapped up in the image we want to project to all those around us. We want people to admire us and give us their approval. We imagine that popularity somehow equals success in our lives, yet Jesus calls His disciples to give up the popularity of the world for the praise of His Father.

Those in the world demand a very high price tag for their approval. They demand our loyalty, require us to agree with their philosophies, accept their moral standards, submit to their politically correct vocabulary, and surrender any convictions that might cause them to feel guilty or uncomfortable in our presence.

After Jesus challenged us to lose our life for Him, He asked "For what will it profit a man if he gains the whole world, and loses his own soul? Or what will a man give in exchange for his soul?" (Matthew 16:26).

God taught me that to die to myself involved exchanging my reputation for His. From that point on, it was no longer important what people thought of me—the only thing that mattered was that others saw Christ in and through me. In the final analysis it really doesn't make any difference whom we please—if we displease the Lord. Nor does it really matter whom we displease, as long as we please the Lord.

After finishing my master's degree, I thought it would be impressive to add a Ph.D. to my name, so I enrolled in a university for this purpose. I was soon aware of the negative influences against my faith in the Lord and in His Word. I felt quite certain, however, that I could withstand such pressures. After all, I'd majored in biblical studies in college and graduate school and memorized extensive passages of the Bible. And beyond that,

I would be commuting from home—where I would also be carrying on youth ministries for which I had been ordained and commissioned.

Early in the first semester I began hearing philosophies that were both biblically and intellectually absurd. A psychology professor declared, "We are all like little boxes. What goes in comes out. So if we want to change behavior, we only have to change the experience."

I raised my hand.

"Are you saying that a person has no will to make moral choices on his or her own?" I asked.

"That's right!" the professor replied. "We are all the products of what we experience. Nothing more."

After several weeks of this training, a certain attitude began growing in my heart—one that I had never expected or anticipated. In spite of earlier resolutions, I found myself nurturing a growing admiration for the prestige of the educational community—and a corresponding disdain for the place of Christians in the world.

This alarmed me. I'd been so sure that I could take these classes without letting them effect me.

One morning on the way to class, I sensed a strong message from God. *Bill, you must make a choice. Either get My approval on your life or man's. Others may have both, but you cannot.* I withdrew from the university and was reassured by the Scripture, "Cease, my son, to hear the instruction that causeth to err from the words of knowledge" (Proverbs 19:27, KJV).

Ceasing to love our life also means rejecting our own ambitions. Recently, I talked with a young man who is a dynamic spiritual leader. Hundreds of teenage boys look up to him as their role model, and their fathers listen to his counsel on training up their sons. I sensed that he was going through some inward struggle, so I asked him what he planned to do in the future.

He said he wanted to go into politics. I responded that God certainly has a place for godly political leaders, but many fail because they go into politics with the goal of self-glorification. I reminded him of the difference between a politician and a true statesman—the first seeks the office, the second is sought out by the office.

Then I quoted a verse that had impacted my life many years before: "But you, are you seeking great things for yourself? Do not seek them" (Jeremiah 45:5, NASB).

"Have you ever dedicated your ambition for political office to God?" I asked him.

"Yes," he replied. "I've put it in God's hands."

"That's the problem," I said. "God doesn't want you to put it in His hands—so you can take it out later. He wants you to put it on the altar and die to it—in the same way that He asked Abraham to put his son on the altar and die to all the dreams he had for his future."

The young man immediately saw the difference and placed all his political ambitions on the altar. The result was a new spiritual power in his life and an increased effectiveness with the young men he was training.

Paul reminded his flock in Colosse to "set your mind on things above, not on things on earth. For you have died, and your life is hidden with Christ in God" (Colossians 3:2–3). Another translation declares, "You died when Christ died…."[4]

Men and women who have truly understood this truth through the centuries have been able to face and overcome their greatest fears. How can you kill someone who has already died? How can you threaten someone whose real and true life is safe forever, beyond reach, in the protective embrace of God's Son? As David wrote, "In God I have put my trust; I will not be afraid. What can man do to me?" (Psalm 56:11).

Let's consider David's question for a moment. What *can* man do to me?

He can take away my earthly possessions. He can mock me and humiliate me. He can exclude me. He can threaten me. He can laugh at me. He can lie about me. He can trump up charges against me. He can arrest me. He can abuse me. He can imprison me. He can starve me. He can kill me. Yet through all this, as Jesus assured us, "Not a hair of your head shall be lost" (Luke 21:18).

Our lives are secure in Him. Our destiny is sealed in heaven. Why should we work so hard to cherish and protect that which can never, never be harmed? Loving our lives here on earth isn't only unbiblical, it is a waste of precious time. Once we receive Jesus Christ as Savior and Lord, everything that ultimately matters has been settled forever.

We are free to live a life that pleases the One who loves us with a jealous love.

POINTS TO PONDER

Read Colossians 3:1–3 and Galatians 2:20. What does Paul mean that we have already died? How might this realization make a difference in the way we view our priorities each day?

Chapter 7

COMPETING AFFECTION #2: LOVING THE WORLD

"You are not of the world, but I chose you out of the world."
JOHN 15:19

Most of us don't wake up in the morning wondering, *Who can I torment today?*

Even so, conflicts still seem to come.

Sometimes we say the wrong thing. At other times, we say the right thing but we're misunderstood. We may not even say anything at all, and *still* be misunderstood. Others form judgments against us or reject us for reasons that never seem clear to us. It's as though the conflicts fall out of the blue sky—or rise up out of the path in front of us just in time to trip us up and make us stumble.

We could say we're "just having a bad day," but does that really explain it? Could it be something more than that?

In a very pointed Scripture, the apostle James wrote: "Where do wars [battles, disputes, or strife] and fights [contentions or quarrels] come from among you? Do they not come from your desires for pleasure that war in your members?" (James 4:1).

Just as God stirred up adversaries against Israel when He saw that they were delighting in a competing affection, so He will do with New Testament believers who try to maintain a friendship with the world—alongside their covenant relationship with Him.

We arouse the jealousy of our Lord…and conflicts become inevitable in our lives.

James leaves no doubt in his words: "Adulterers and adulteresses! Do you not know that friendship with the world is enmity with God? Whoever therefore wants to be a friend of the world makes himself an enemy of God" (James 4:4).

There is no way to love the Lord with all of our heart

if we have a competing love with the world. It would be like a married man putting up a photo of another woman on his desk at work, alongside a portrait of his wife. It's offensive! It doesn't belong! For this reason, Scripture pleads with us, "Do not love the world or the things in the world. If anyone loves the world, the love of the Father is not in him. For all that is in the world—the lust of the flesh, the lust of the eyes, and the pride of life—is not of the Father but is of the world. And the world is passing away, and the lust of it; but he who does the will of God abides forever" (1 John 2:15–17).

This list describes all too clearly the daily assaults of today's culture. In such an atmosphere, we can certainly not be passive or neutral. We must be committed to loving God and being hated by the world—or loving the world and being an enemy of God. Much as we might like to think so at times, there really is no middle ground.

Scripture defines the three categories that make up the "world" in illuminating detail.

THE LUST OF THE FLESH

"The lust of the flesh" involves longings for that which is forbidden and leads to the following sins: "Adultery, fornication, uncleanness, lewdness, idolatry, sorcery, hatred, contentions, jealousies, outbursts of wrath, selfish ambitions, dissensions, heresies, envy, murders, drunkenness, revelries, and the like; of which I tell you beforehand, just as I also told you in time past, that those who practice such things will not inherit the kingdom of God" (Galatians 5:19–21).

If we claim that we are against such things as adultery, fornication, and uncleanness—but invest our money, time, and attention on movies, music, books, and magazines that describe, portray, and glorify these activities, then we are guilty of loving the world. That view may not be popular these days—even in Christian circles. But when you stop to think about it…how could it be otherwise?

THE LUST OF THE EYE

"The lust of the eye" involves greed for things that please our sensual desires. Such greed is never satisfied because it is outside the will of God. It is only by knowing Christ in an intimate way and experiencing His resurrection power that we find deep and lasting satisfaction in our lives.

Paul understood this when he made the decision to exchange temporal things for eternal treasures. He stated, "Yet indeed I also count all things loss for the excellence of the knowledge of Christ Jesus my Lord, for whom I have suffered the loss of all things, and count them as rubbish, that I may gain Christ" (Philippians 3:8).

If we serve the lust of our eyes, we will have a futile existence, because "Hell and Destruction are never full; so the eyes of man are never satisfied" (Proverbs 27:20).

Attracting our attention with the lust of the eyes has been Satan's program from the beginning. The forbidden fruit was pleasant to the eyes of Eve; Delilah pleased Samson's eyes; and Bathsheba delighted David's eyes.

Choosing to love the world is deciding to enjoy pleasures that appeal to our carnal nature, regardless of how they may damage other people—especially our spouse, our children, and our fellow believers. Paul used the church controversy over meat offered to idols to explain how we are to do nothing that might cause a fellow believer to stumble, become weak, or be offended (Romans 14:21).

If there are conflicts with other people over the things we allow in our lives, we must ask ourselves, "Is this an evidence given by God that I have a competing affection which is grieving His Spirit?"

As God's champion, Daniel successfully resisted the lure and the love of the world and experienced the unimagined rewards of God's favor. Scripture reveals the secret that he used to conquer the world. *He made vows ahead of time, to prepare for the worldly temptations that he anticipated would come.*

When Daniel realized he knew he would be taken captive into Babylon, he "made up his mind that he would not defile himself with the king's choice food or with the wine which he drank" (Daniel 1:8, NASB).

As a high school student, I was concerned about the positive publicity the newspapers were giving to a well-known sensual magazine. I knew it would popularize pornography and damage millions of lives and marriages. I made a vow that I would never look inside one of these magazines. That was over fifty years ago. God has been faithful to both remove the desire for it and protect me from it.

THE BOASTFUL PRIDE OF LIFE

The third aspect of "love of the world" from 1 John 2 is described as "the boastful pride of life."

Men, in particular, take pride in their occupations. "What I do" seems to be an important part of "Who I am." When I was in high school, I watched my dad weather a job crisis where he deliberately turned his back on the "boastful pride of life" in order to please the Lord.

After twenty years of faithful service to his engineering publishing company, my father was offered the top job in the whole firm. He was invited to become the company president.

What an ego boost that must have been for him—as it would have been for almost anyone. But there was one hitch. Before the contract was signed, the current president, who would become the chairman of the board, gave one final requirement: he wanted my father to promote a certain product in the magazine.

My father instantly realized that this product was associated with evil and corruption and that he could not participate in advertising it. He explained his convictions to the president of the company, and also stated that if this was required, he would have to assume that his work with the company was over.

I saw my father walk away from a very high paying job, with many extra benefits. He had no job in sight and six children to support. Though I was only a teenager at the time, I will never forget my father's first action after resigning. To me, it was a courageous step of faith. He immediately cashed in one of his securities and sent a large gift to a missionary in Germany.

As I saw him make these kinds of sacrifices, I determined that if he could do it in the business world, I could do it in my high school. After several months, my father became the executive director of Gideons International—an organization that places Bibles in hotels and other places. He also became the chairman of the board of the Pacific Garden Mission, and was instrumental in launching the Christian radio drama, *Unshackled*.

Gideons International has a worldwide ministry of distributing up to one million Bibles a week. *Unshackled* is now the longest running radio drama in history, broadcast day and night across the globe. Meanwhile, a few years after he left, the engineering publishing company went out of business.

Reflecting on this incident reminds me of the words of David:

> Who is the man who fears the LORD?
> He will instruct him in the way he should choose.
> PSALM 25:12, NASB

Because of my father's obedient choices, because he chose to value the fear of the Lord over the love of the world, God guided him into ministries that have reached around the world. And beyond that, his young son was watching him make those choices...and they have marked me and my ministry through all the years of my life.

POINTS TO PONDER

I wrote about the impact of my father's choices on my life as a young high school student. Who might be watching your life today, observing your decisions as you choose between loving Christ and loving the world?

Chapter 8

COMPETING AFFECTION #3: LOVING MONEY

"For where your treasure is, there your heart will be also."
MATTHEW 6:21

Whatever controls our money controls our heart.

For this reason, God has a special jealousy over our attitude toward money. He knows that the "those who want to get rich fall into temptation and a snare and many foolish and harmful desires which plunge men into ruin and destruction" (1 Timothy 6:9, NASB).

I learned one of my first lessons on the eternal value of

money as a young teenager at a youth banquet in Chicago. One of the speakers explained how a "faith promise" offering works, and it was the first time I'd ever encountered the term. He encouraged us to write down on a card an amount of money that we would trust God to provide for us each month—over and above what we expected to receive. As a thirteen-year-old school boy, almost anything I got was more than I expected, so I wrote down an amount which certainly seemed like a lot of money to me!

To my amazement, the money was always there by the end of every month. It came from unexpected jobs, the sale of unused items, or outright gifts. At the end of the year, I had sent in the full amount of my faith promise.

Then God did the unexpected. He worked out circumstances so that I received a gift of exactly twice the amount I had given away!

TRY ME NOW IN THIS...

A few years later, I opened my first savings account and began tucking away every dollar I could earn. By the time I was a sophomore in high school I was very pleased with the balance in my little beige bankbook. In fact, I was more than pleased. I was proud. I wondered how many other students had as much money in the bank as I did. Gazing at the balance in that bank book somehow made me feel more important and self-sufficient.

God, who jealously watches the hearts of all His children, knew exactly how I felt…and decided to do something about it.

One Sunday morning I was sitting in church listening to a guest speaker from the Gideon's. He told how they placed Bibles in hotels and hospitals and gave away New Testaments to tens of thousands of school children. Idly, with no real intention of doing anything about it, I calculated how many New Testaments I could buy with all of the money I had in the bank.

Suddenly God interrupted my musing with a convicting message from Scripture: "Do not lay up for yourselves treasures on earth, where moth and rust destroy and where thieves break in and steal; but lay up for yourselves treasures in heaven, where neither moth nor rust destroys and where thieves do not break in and steal. For where your treasure is, there your heart will be also" (Matthew 6:19–21).

I thought about how my treasure and my heart were both securely held in the First National Bank of LaGrange. On the heels of this upsetting thought, God troubled me with another passage of Scripture: "Will a man rob God?" (Malachi 3:8).

Horrors no!, I thought.

"Yet you have robbed Me! …In tithes and offerings."

It suddenly dawned on me that I had never tithed that money in my account. The passage continues:

"Bring all the tithes into the storehouse,
That there may be food in My house,
And try Me now in this,"
Says the LORD of hosts,
"If I will not open for you the windows of heaven
And pour out for you such blessing
That there will not be room enough to receive it."

MALACHI 3:10

I began to bargain with God: "Lord, I'll give You 10 percent of that bank account." That didn't seem to impress Him—or me. So I said, "I'll give You half of all of the money." But then the words from Malachi came surging back into my mind... *Try Me now in this.... If I will not open for you the windows of heaven.*

Finally, I decided to give God my bank account. The whole thing. This meant the death to my vision of buying a car. Yet I was even more excited about proving God's faithfulness. When I gave the money to God, I was not expecting Him to give money in return. Instead, I wanted Him to give me more faith. With faith, I knew I would be able to acquire whatever I needed to carry out God's will for my life.

In the coming days, however, unexpected opportunities to earn money began to roll in. A metallurgist asked if I would develop and print pictures of highly magnified steel in my home photo lab, so that he could tell what types of alloys they contained. He paid me very well for this after-school job and by the next year I had twice the amount of money in the bank that I had given away—plus a car that was better than the one that I could have purchased the year before!

You would think that with experiences like these any love of money would be conquered. But God knew that my secret affection for money had deep roots, and that I had some important further lessons to learn.

FURTHER TESTING

One day, I climbed into my prized '58 Chevy to drive to a nearby village. I was thinking about the new bank account I had started, and relishing the fact that I was again beginning to rack up the savings.

At almost the same instant, a thought popped into my mind. *What if you have an accident with this car?* Suddenly, I realized that if God took His hand of protection off of me for one moment, all my hard-earned money would vanish.

I decided to be very careful to be certain that I wouldn't have an accident. As I approached a row of parallel parked cars in our business district, I slowly crept by them, so that I wouldn't run into any that might back out quickly. Then down the road, I noticed the flashing red light of a police car. There must have been an accident! Driving up on that scene, I turned my attention to the damaged car. When I looked back to the road, the car in front of me had stopped. With sickening certainty, I realized I would not be able to brake in time. A few seconds later, I crashed into the bumper of that car.

I sat there in disbelief, looking at my beloved Chevy's crinkled hood and the steam pouring out of the damaged radiator. But even in that distressing moment, I was conscious of the presence of the Lord. A verse of Scripture popped into my mind: "For whom the LORD loves He chastens, and scourges every son whom He receives" (Hebrews 12:6).

My car was still drivable, so I reluctantly headed to a body shop for an estimate on the repair cost. The amount was a powerful message from the Lord. *It was exactly the amount of my new bank account*—to the very dollar!

God used many other experiences to prove His ability to provide for all my needs if I first gave Him full control of my money. It was just as His Word promises, "Give, and it will be given to you. They will pour into your lap a good measure—pressed down, shaken together, and running over. For by your standard of measure it will be measured to you in return" (Luke 6:38, NASB).

A STORY OF LOST GOLD

My final exam on finances came when I was thirty years old, during my forty-day fast in the Northwoods. In the middle of that very precious time, I noticed an end table and wondered what was in the drawer. Inside was an old *Life* magazine. I opened it up to a feature article about a scuba diving instructor in Costa Rica.

One day he was waiting for a student to arrive and decided to swim out to a coral reef. As he climbed over the reef, he noticed something glittering about fifteen feet down in the clear water. He dove down and brought up a handful of gold coins.

Centuries earlier, a Spanish galleon had been ripped open during a storm and spilled its treasures alongside the reef. The treasure had laid there undiscovered all of those years—eleven million dollars worth of gold. A strong wave of envy and greed surged over my soul. I thought, *Why couldn't I have discovered that gold?*

At that important moment in my life, God brought me to a point of decision. Was I going to focus on money so that I could be rich or was I going to seek after God's kingdom and lay up eternal treasures? In a very definitive prayer, I told the Lord that I would never heap up riches for myself, but would live as frugally as I could so that I might give as much as possible to Him.

There is a significant ending to the treasure story. Several years later, some friends paid my way to Jamaica. During the trip, I met an old sailor and struck up a conversation. When I learned that he came from Costa Rica, I asked him if he knew the scuba diving instructor who had discovered the gold. He said that he knew him very well.

"Whatever happened to him?" I asked.

The weathered old seaman looked up at me through bushy eyebrows. "It's a tragic story," he replied. Then he began to recount it to me.

In order to keep the find a secret, the diver would work at night, gathering bags of gold that had been encrusted in the coral reef. He used gallons of acid to extract the coins from the coral. The next morning, he and a relative would take the bags to the bank to put them in a vault. Unsuspecting neighbors would say to him, "What do you have there, bags of gold?" Then they would smile and laugh.

But one day someone discovered his secret, and soon the word was out. The government claimed that the money was theirs and stationed a boat over the site. Scuba divers came from everywhere and swam under the boat and brought back their share of the treasures. Friends and relatives demanded money from the man and problems erupted with his wife. The old sailor ended by saying, "Today that man is penniless, divorced, in poor health, and depressed."

It was like the Lord was saying to me, *Bill, the decision you made when you were thirty years old was the right decision. I will entrust to you much more than that man discovered. It will not be for you. It will be provided for you to share the true riches of My Word to the world and to demonstrate My love through giving.*

To reject the love of money is to experience the words of the proverb: "The blessing of the LORD makes one rich, and He adds no sorrow with it" (Proverbs 10:22). During the past four months alone, God has provided for this ministry an amount much greater than what that scuba diver discovered!

God is jealous over the competing affection of money for good reason. It not only becomes a god and idol in our lives, but it is a particularly cruel and demanding taskmaster. Paul reminded Timothy that "the love of money is a root of all kinds of evil, for which some have strayed from the faith in their greediness, and pierced themselves through with many sorrows" (1 Timothy 6:10).

Our loving Shepherd doesn't want us to stray from the faith...to wander away from His protective care. He doesn't want us to fall into the thorn bushes of greed and financial preoccupation, where the more we struggle, the more we strive, the more we are wounded.

He's jealous to guard us from such sorrow, as we might expect.

A good God is only jealous for our good.

POINTS TO PONDER

Our Lord, who knows the future and knows our hearts, is jealous of the influence of money in shaping our lives and marking our critical life decisions. Could this chapter be God's loving warning to you to rethink your current directions and priorities?

JEALOUS FOR
EACH OTHER

*And let us consider one another in order to
stir up love and good works, not forsaking
the assembling of ourselves together,
as is the manner of some, but exhorting one another,
and so much the more as you see the Day approaching.*
HEBREWS 10:24–25

As I look back over the years of my life, some of the people
I am most grateful for are those who challenged me to love
and serve our Lord.

My parents were constant mentors and examples for
doing what was right, as were my two older sisters. One

seemed almost omnipresent. Whenever I was about to do something wrong, she was there. She was jealous for my good, and though I didn't always appreciate it then, I love her for it now.

I'm grateful for pastors, colleagues, and friends who have loved me and exhorted me and prayed for me. I'm grateful for my critics, who have sent me back to the Word of God (and back to my knees!) again and again to sharpen and refine my message.

The writer of Hebrews challenges his readers: "See to it that no one comes short of the grace of God…that there be no immoral or godless person like Esau, who sold his own birthright for a single meal" (Hebrews 12:15, 16, NASB).

See to it! Encourage, teach, exhort, nudge one another to love the Lord with heart, soul, mind, and strength. Be jealous, as God is jealous, for the joy of your brothers and sisters and their success and growth in the Lord Jesus Christ.

That's the way it was in my family with my sister.

That's the way it is in any family that cares for each other.

That's the way it is in the family of God, where our Father and our Elder Brother have shown the way.